MICROGREENS

---

*A Few Simple Steps to Grow Gourmet Greens
at Home*

Antony Land

Copyright © by Antony Land

All rights reserved. No part of this book may be reproduced or used in any form without the express written permission of the publisher except for the use of brief quotation in a book review.

First Printing 2020

Auto Biography

Hi, my name is Antony Land, an expert in greenhouse cultivation. My father, who I had been helping in the family business since I was a boy, passed on this passion to me. Over the years, I have perfected its production techniques, refining them with the knowledge of modern technologies. It was not easy to find the perfect formulas in hydroponic cultivation. But after years of research and experimentation I am ready to share with you the secrets that make my company a successful business, in fact I have been collaborating for years with the largest food distribution chains in the Québec, where I live with my family, who supports me in my business.

Table of Contents

Introduction

In the course of recent years, enthusiasm for nearby, crisp, and natural nourishment has been on the ascent. There has been a restoration of the little homestead and a reestablishment of thankfulness for new vegetables. The recovery of the rancher's showcase, the commencement of the CSA model (Community Supported Agriculture), and the general development towards perfect, entire nourishments has been phenomenal and is proceeding to develop.

Individuals are rediscovering the significance of crisp, privately developed nourishment. This development has indicated that it isn't only for the well-to-do, for those keen on cultivating, yet for the entire of the populace and people in the future.

With their capacity to highlight and develop our association with nature, we accept that microgreens have a spot in the developing enthusiasm of nourishment. Reaped from the get-go in their lives, microgreens are delicate, sensitive, and exceptionally delightful. They have a fresh yet liquefy in-your-mouth surface and an assortment of flavors that swing from sweet to appetizing to gritty to hot. Toss in the abundant excellence of their reds, yellows, greens, and purples and you have a plate of mixed greens that is unadulterated pleasure.

With the entirety of the shifted tastes and surfaces, incorporating microgreens into your eating regimen can be fun and simple. Leaving on this Endeavor of developing and eating your own greens doesn't necessitate that you change your eating regimen. Stuffed with extraordinary taste, these little greens can be added to pretty much anything. Eaten alone as a serving of mixed greens or added to soups, entrées, sandwiches, burgers, or whatever else you can envision, microgreens will improve your nourishment and your life.

In the course of recent years, microgreens have picked up prominence as a hot new culinary pattern. From New York to Los Angeles, gourmet experts have been getting a charge out of them as an approach to inventively emphasize plates of nourishment and add new profundities of flavor to their dishes. While this pattern has grown, a chosen few producer has exploited this specialty showcase. Indeed, even in metropolitan center points, where gourmet specialists can purchase the majority of their produce from ranchers' markets, a great part of the microgreens advertise has been ruled via mail request.

Chapter #1
Microgreens

Microgreens for Commercial Grower:

Growing microgreens is a method for extending the extent of your activity to incorporate this to a great extent undiscovered market. We have never demonstrated our greens to a culinary expert who wasn't amped up for utilizing them. This energy is shifting into the customer showcase too, making request considerably more grounded. As an ever-increasing number of individuals are encountering the subjective contrast of crisp neighbourhood produce, your microgreens will sell without any problem. Offering your locale this all year asset can be an incredible method to enhance your activity. Another advantage these greens offer is their capacity to get speedy ranch salary while likewise adding to its ripeness.

On numerous farms it frequently takes at any rate several months to begin recovering the cash put resources into fertilized soils and manures. While the little ranch's essential spotlight isn't as a rule on making a buck yet rather the soundness of the land and its encompassing network, consistent salary is fundamental to addressing the necessities of the homestead and ranch family.

Microgreens require negligible starting venture, with most assortments costing under two dollars for every plate for seed and soil. When planted, they can begin creating pay in only a little while.

After your plate have been gathered, fertilizing the soil your dirt presently loaded up with stem and root matter is likewise fast and simple. In the warmth of the mid-year this dirt can be revised, treated the soil, and prepared to use in less than a month. We have made an uncommon worm container for this reason. As our plate are treated the soil, a lot of worm castings are added to the dirt, advancing it much further. Now it very well may be utilized to begin your seedlings, consolidated into your fields, or even used to develop more microgreens. With the entirety of their favourable circumstances, you can perceive any reason why microgreens can upgrade the little ranch.

For Home Grower:
Adjacent to their extraordinary taste and classy interest, microgreens are also unimaginably nutritious. The ability to accumulate and eat them inside minutes gives you access to their most restoratively rich state. They give us a strong bit of palatable supplements, minerals, and phytonutrients. While your taste buds benefit as much as possible from their extraordinary flavour, your body will get the compensations of their concentrated enhancements.

It's a remarkable thing to eat something so incredible that you get goose bumps from how brilliant and alive it is. We have been growing and eating microgreen plates of blended greens for a significant long time and still the general thought of fixing one for ourselves puts favours our faces. We are continually astounded at the sum we can eat at once; it's like drinking an infection glass of water on a rankling summer's day. Your body is in completed simultaneousness with your cerebrum that this, right now, is essentially the best thing you could give.

Children and Microgreens:

Growing microgreens isn't only for grown-ups! It tends to be an enjoyment and simple path for kids to interface with nature. Microgreens give a connecting with venture at home or at school, instructing about where nourishment originates from and how to develop it. Youngsters have all the more an association with things on the off chance that they are a piece of the procedure. Seeds become their seeds that develop into their greens. A personality and association are shaped with the plants and their advancement. Molly Kaizen portrayed this marvel when she discussed taking a gathering of school children to "The Pizza Farm" in northern California. The children invested energy watching and finding out pretty much the entirety of the segments that made up pizza; the cows that created the milk that made the cheddar, the fields that developed the wheat that they ground into flour to make the outside layer, and the growing herbs and tomatoes that made up the sauce. At that point, they made their own pizza. She portrayed the expectation as they trusted that their pizza will wrap up; every one checking each couple of minutes to check whether their magnum opuses were finished. This fervour doesn't occur while our little one's trust that solidified pizza will show up on their plates. It is a blessing to give our kids a consciousness of their nourishment and its procedure. Particularly in rural and urban regions, numerous youngsters today aren't exactly certain where nourishment originates from.

In the event that one has never observed a carrot collected out of the earth, how might you realize that is the place it originated from? It could be similarly as intelligent that a carrot originates from a can or basically from the store. Beginning microgreens with your kids allows them to get their hands in the earth. It offers them the chance to find what else is growing in the dirt. It gets alive in their brains, as they watch worms separate their kitchen scraps or seeds spring to life. You may even locate your critical eaters requesting more greens on their supper plates! When this living world has been proposed, the conceivable outcomes are unfathomable. From a couple of straightforward seeds come fresh out of the box new eyes for nature.

Microgreens vs. Sprouts vs. Baby Greens:
Sprouts, microgreens, and child greens are on the whole stages in a plant's advancement. Every ha distinguishing attributes and fluctuating dietary benefits. A grow is the primary phase of a seed's advancement. "Sprout" is really synonymous with germination. Developed in various sorts of compartments, these seeds are kept soggy and at room temperature until they sprout. Rather than permitting them to develop in a medium and set up into a plant, grows are expended directly after they sprout. Regularly somewhat obscure and yielding a crunchy surface, they have gotten progressively famous for their healthy benefit.

At the point when developed in a medium (soil or something else), the second phase of a seed's advancement includes the foundation of its underlying foundations and the opening of its first leaves, called cotyledons. Greens reaped at this stage are called microgreens. On the off chance that microgreens are permitted to keep on growing, they put on their next arrangement of leaves, called "genuine leaves." True leaves are the leaves of a plant that recognize it from another plant. While numerous brassicas (cabbage, broccoli, arugula, and so on.) all have fundamentally the same as heart-formed cotyledons, when their actual leaves create, they look very changed and are handily recognized from one another. These greens are collected in their early stages, and are just permitted to develop in the dirt for up to 14 days. They have the entirety of the medical advantages of sprouts with the additional bit of leeway of follow minerals raised from the dirt they are developed in. At this stage their surface, appearance, and flavour are significantly more like a plate of mixed greens green than a crunchy grow. In the event that the seed were permitted to keep on growing past the genuine leaf stage and, given enough reality, it would inevitably arrive at the infant green stage. Child greens are delicate leaves that are well known in plate of mixed greens blends frequently called mesclun or spring blend. They are tastier and more delicate than leaves from a full-developed head of lettuce however lose a portion of the power of flavour and healthy benefit that they had at the microgreen organize.

Health and Microgreens:

As individuals, our fundamental establishments lie in the soil. But countless us have disregarded this noteworthy association over the span of the last barely any ages, our relationship with nature is so out of date and fundamental that it can't be completely excused. In case while we are eating, we take a short relief, we can without quite a bit of a stretch follow our sustenance back to the plants, the animals, the soil, and even the breeze, deluge, and sun. These things have their combination on the property. There is no avoiding that the adequacy of the earth and the prosperity of people are by and by tied.

Standard agriculture has been practiced for an enormous number of years wherever all through the world. Little extension and worked by hand, these farms are significantly widened and capably tended. Widened farmers make the craft of soil stewardship their basic work, developing in a way that truly adds to and improves the life of the estate and everything and everyone that interfaces with it. The animals raised here are alert with strong coats. The earth is rich, diminish, and sweet smelling. The plants are rich and grow vivaciously with negligible sign of pressure. The sustenance become here contributes evening out and prosperity to its incorporating system. To be sure, even the typical onlooker can see that "baffling something" that overruns the air around such a farm.

The greater a residence is in scale and the greater its mechanical objectives, the further it meanders from this separated little farm model. All through the main residual century there has been a persistent move in the scale and point of convergence of the farm at this moment. Prior to the completion of World War II, it was regularly envisioned that bleeding edge, mechanized mechanical structures were better than little extension customary methodologies. Close by industrialization came the beginning of substance fertilizer use in cultivating. After the war, an impressive parcel of the heightens that were used in the formation of bombs were changed into plant manures.

During this time, conviction that farms ought to have been gigantic to misuse the modern office hypothesis got hold. Various farmers got off the land and into the urban networks to join the growing example of industry. The family farm steadily evaporated as huge agri-business got hold.

Throughout the main outstanding century, the United States has lost over 4.5 million farms. As demonstrated by the U.S.

specification office, the degree of people living and tackling farms has gone from 40 percent to under 1 percent. Close by this revamping of our nation's farms came the unpreventable exchange off of the idea of produce available. In Paul Bergner's book, The Healing Power of Minerals, Special Nutrients and Trace Elements, USDA estimations are consolidated that speak to this lessening. These figures show mineral and supplement substance declining in a couple of sorts of results of the dirt between the years 1962 and 1992. Among others, calcium dropped by pretty much 30 percent, iron by 32 percent, and magnesium by 21 percent. Produce sustenance is compelled by the idea of soil it was created, by the way it was procured, its treatment after gather, and how old it is once it shows up at your fork. To get a sentiment of how nutritious microgreens are, we ought to at first look at how these components impact the healthy substance of our produce.

Health and Soil:

The collaborations among plants and soil are so immense and complex that a few people have devoted their whole lives to contemplate them. From these investigations, researchers are reaffirming what the conventional rancher has known for a large number of years; assorted variety is one of the keys to sound soil and thusly solid plants and animals. Yield turns, manures, soil corrections, supportable creature cultivation, and the growing of a wide assortment of vegetables all join into the extending decent variety and ripeness of the land. Produce developed in prolific ground can get a bounty of phytonutrients, minerals, and follow components. An attention on the strength of soil science prompts natural vermin and dry season obstruction, making a ranch that can support life inconclusively.

In ordinary horticulture, soil has become only a medium that holds our vegetables upstanding rather than the living, powerful power that it ought to be. Right now, soil the executives is viewed as in-effective and second rate. Centre, rather, is put for huge scope single-crop creation (mono-culture) and expansive range compound treatment. Within this framework, the tremendous measure of soil-improving systems is overlooked and supplanted with persistent uses of three water-dissolvable composts: nitrogen, phosphorus, and potassium (N-P-K). Natural life in the dirt is incredibly diminished, bargaining its wellbeing and respectability.

When this issue has started underneath the surface, indications start to emerge in the plant bodies. Out of nowhere the plant's characteristic protection from bugs, parasite, and ailment has been undermined, leaving it open and defenceless against assault. This issue is treated in ordinary agribusiness with the use of a wide scope of pesticides and fungicides. The outcomes appear to be successful. Less bugs, less illness, less generally speaking harm to the plant. To the unaided eye, the dirt despite everything looks dark coloured and the plant despite everything looks green. It appears to be a proficient, viable technique for controlling these undesirable factors.

Tragically, as the dirt keeps on being disregarded, vegetables are given heavier and heavier uses of these poisonous substances. In the end the synthetic concoctions must be unsafe to the point that unique suits and veils should be utilized to apply them. Now, if you somehow happened to investigate the surface, you would see the loss of organic life and the possible passing of the dirt. When the entirety of the microbial life has been executed, no measure of nitrogen, phosphorus, or potassium can bring it back. Soil that was once rich and fruitful gets inadmissible for farming. The dirt has become something to treat as opposed to something to construct and reinforce. This is reflected in the manner that cutting-edge medication thinks about the human body. Much time is spent tending to a patient's manifestations instead of taking a gander at the reason. As infections are getting more grounded, so are bugs. We continue expanding the measurements just to find that the foundation of the issue despite everything exists and the indications are getting increasingly hard to treat. Some have discovered an increasingly all-encompassing methodology—taking a gander at the entire body, the entire ranch, the entire earth—to be the answer for both human wellbeing and agribusiness. It is getting increasingly more of a standard thought that sound nourishment and a functioning way of life help with the life span and soundness of people.

Health and Harvesting:

The joint efforts among plants and soil are so monstrous and complex that a couple of individuals have dedicated their entire lives to mull over them. From these examinations, scientists are reaffirming what the customary farmer has known for countless years; grouped assortment is one of the keys to sound soil and in this manner strong plants and animals. Yield turns, composts, soil remedies, supportable animal development, and the growing of a wide collection of vegetables all join into the broadening not too bad assortment and readiness of the land. Produce created in productive ground can get an abundance of phytonutrients, minerals, and follow segments. A consideration on the quality of soil science prompts regular vermin and dry season hindrance, making a farm that can bolster life uncertainly.

In conventional cultivation, soil has become just a medium that holds our vegetables upstanding instead of the living, amazing force that it should be. At the present time, soil the administrators is seen as in-viable and below average. Focus, rather, is put for gigantic extension single-crop creation (monoculture) and far reaching range compound treatment. Inside this structure, the huge proportion of soil-improving frameworks are neglected and displaced with diligent employments of three water-dissolvable manures: nitrogen, phosphorus, and potassium (N-P-K). Common life in the soil is unimaginably reduced, bartering its prosperity and decency.

At the point when this issue has begun underneath the surface, signs begin to develop in the plant bodies. Out of the blue the plant's trademark assurance from bugs, parasite, and affliction has been undermined, leaving it open and vulnerable against ambush. This issue is treated in common agribusiness with the utilization of a wide extent of pesticides and fungicides. The results seem, by all accounts, to be effective. Less bugs, less sickness, less as a rule mischief to the plant. To the independent eye, the earth notwithstanding everything looks dull shaded and the plant regardless of everything looks green. It gives off an impression of being a capable, feasible procedure for controlling these unfortunate components.

Shockingly, as the earth continues being ignored, vegetables are given heavier and heavier employments of these harmful substances. At last the engineered creations must be dangerous to the point that special suits and shroud ought to be used to apply them. Presently, on the off chance that you some way or another happened to research the surface, you would see the loss of natural life and the conceivable going of the soil.

At the point when the total of the microbial life has been executed, no proportion of nitrogen, phosphorus, or potassium can bring it back. Soil that was once rich and productive gets forbidden for cultivating. The soil has become something to treat instead of something to build and strengthen. This is reflected in the way that bleeding edge prescription contemplates the human body. Much time is burned through watching out for a patient's signs as opposed to looking at the explanation. As contaminations are getting more grounded, so are bugs. We keep extending the estimations just to find that the establishment of the issue regardless of everything exists and the signs are getting progressively difficult to treat. Some have found an undeniably widely inclusive system—looking at the whole body, the whole farm, the whole earth—to be the response for both human prosperity and agribusiness. It is getting progressively to a greater degree a standard idea that sound sustenance and a working lifestyle help with the life expectancy and adequacy of individuals.

Nutritional Independence and Microgreens:

The joint endeavours among plants and soil are so colossal and complex that two or three people have committed their whole lives to think about them. From these assessments, researchers are reaffirming what the standard rancher has known for innumerable years; gathered variety is one of the keys to sound soil and right now plants and animals. Yield turns, fertilizers, soil cures, supportable creature advancement, and the growing of a wide assortment of vegetables all join into the widening not all that awful combination and preparation of the land. Produce made in gainful ground can get a plenitude of phytonutrients, minerals, and follow fragments. A thought on the nature of soil science prompts standard vermin and dry season impediment, making a ranch that can reinforce life uncertainly.

In traditional development, soil has become only a medium that holds our vegetables upstanding rather than the living, astonishing power that it ought to be. Right now, soil the overseers is viewed as in-reasonable and beneath normal. Centre, rather, is put for monstrous expansion single-crop creation (mono-culture) and broad range compound treatment. Inside this structure, the immense extent of soil-improving systems is dismissed and dislodged with persevering occupations of three water-dissolvable excrements: nitrogen, phosphorus, and potassium (N-P-K). Normal life in the dirt is incredibly decreased, bargaining its success and conventionality.

Right when this issue has started underneath the surface, signs start to create in the plant bodies. Out of nowhere the plant's trademark confirmation from bugs, parasite, and torment has been undermined, leaving it open and powerless against trap. This issue is treated in like manner agribusiness with the use of a wide degree of pesticides and fungicides. The outcomes appear, apparently, to be successful. Less bugs, less affliction, less generally speaking insidiousness to the plant. To the autonomous eye, the earth despite everything looks dull concealed and the plant paying little mind to everything looks green. It radiates an impression of being an able, doable strategy for controlling these heartbreaking parts.

Incredibly, as the earth keeps being overlooked, vegetables are given heavier and heavier vocations of these destructive substances. Finally, the designed manifestations must be risky to the point that exceptional suits and cover should be utilized to apply them. By and by, if you somehow happened to inquire about the surface, you would see the loss of common life and the possible going of the dirt. Right when the aggregate of the microbial life has been executed, no extent of nitrogen, phosphorus, or potassium can bring it back. Soil that was once rich and gainful gets prohibited for developing. The dirt has become something to treat as opposed to something to manufacture and reinforce. This is reflected in the manner that front line solution thinks about the human body. Much time is consumed keeping an eye out for a patient's signs rather than taking a gander at the clarification. As pollutions are getting more grounded, so are bugs. We continue stretching out the estimations just to find that the foundation of the issue paying little mind to everything exists and the signs are getting dynamically hard to treat. Some have discovered an evidently broadly comprehensive framework taking a gander at the entire body, the entire ranch, the entire earth to be the reaction for both human thriving and agribusiness. It is getting continuously to a more prominent degree a standard thought that sound sustenance and a working way of life help with the future and sufficiency of people.

Cruciferous Vegetables and Cancer Prevention:
There have been innumerable examinations done demonstrating the connection between malignancy counteraction and the utilization of cruciferous vegetables (i.e.,

all brassicas: broccoli, cabbage, arugula, and so on.). The crystalline mixes (indoles) found in cruciferous vegetables have a scope of medical advantages. Studies have indicated a huge decrease of instances of lung, bosom, colon, ovarian, and bladder malignant growth in individuals who eat an eating routine high in these vegetables. They contain an estrogen stabilizer, diindolylmethane (DIM), which is significant for the two people. The parity that this compound makes brings about more noteworthy protection from malignant growth just as the consolation of generally hormone balance. Malignancy development can be prodded by certain estrogen metabolites dynamic in the body. Diminish goes about as a deactivator, halting development. There has likewise been broad research done on the impacts of the phytonutrient sulforaphane, which is additionally inexhaustible in cruciferous vegetables. This amazing phytonutrient helps in detoxification, kicking off the liver's common inclination to flush the framework. Lamentably, it is difficult to expend the amounts of cruciferous vegetables expected to receive the rewards. Enter microgreens. Studies have indicated that one-and-a-half cups of full-developed broccoli has a similar measure of this phytonutrient as only one ounce of broccoli four days after it has sprouted. It is accepted that the youthful broccoli has twenty to fifty-fold the amount of sulforaphane as the completely developed.

Chapter 2
Pea Shoots, Sunflower Shoots, and Popcorn Shoots

Sometime around the middle of February, it seems to hit the weariness of satisfying my shopping basket using fresh veggies from California, Chile, Mexico, as well as Peru or New Zealand. No crime to the rocky farmers across the U.S. and around the Earth, since I genuinely appreciate the chance to eat apples through a snowstorm. However, these products need, by requirement, prolonged shipping times that sap them of taste and nourishment to a level. Nonetheless, it is not simple to consume local once you reside in a spot that needs budgeting 20 minutes each morning to scraping the ice from the windshield. The only way it could be completed in a little way is to grow that which you could inside, or tap to anything canning and dehydrating you achieved the summertime.

Because we are inclined to run from our food preservation concessions by March at our residence, we prompted us to start experimenting with easy-to-grow options, which led right into shoots.

Unlike Illness --that are increased in water and need meticulous scheduling for rinsing and maintenance to steer clear of bacterial problems --fires have been grown in the dirt;

therefore, it is a cinch to become flexible concerning time, resource use, distance, and other significant facets. We started growing them only to find out what could happen, and our small farm is turning into a provider of shoots local restaurants--among them has dubbed a pea-shoot-laden veggie dish that the "Bossy Burger." Who would not wish to eat this? Likely, you will not start growing shoots such a vast scale, which you need to offer them from the pound to nearby eateries, but something is addicting about watching those shoots appear so fast.

The pea shoots possess a soul-quenching pinch and a delicate taste that tastes like spring up, anytime. Sunflower shoots are succulent, with a feel that is surprisingly firm also holds up nicely in a sauté. Popcorn shoots our main experiment whatsoever, is superbly peculiar in their own best. They seem somewhat like wheatgrass, however, flavor like quite youthful candy corn, then strike one with the aftertaste of corn stalk. I tend to combine all of the shoots to bargain with that amazing aftertaste, but a few folks have told me that they currently crave that taste. With these three options, shoots will be just a couple weeks away from flourishing under your lights, so let us begin.

Excellent Options for Growing Shoots

Overall, shoots are just microgreens of those seeds you have selected. Consequently, if you should allow the peas, sunflowers, and peppermint to develop into full adulthood, you would have those crops. But since you harvest them at this young age, the flavors are more extreme, and you'll be able to plant them closer together in a set tray. Together with shoots, assortment does not often matter very far, but I have found better outcomes with a particular sort of pea seed. Here are some options:

- Dwarf Grey Sugar' peas: Following far experimentation, we currently utilize just those, possibly for our plantation and also for home growing. They are designed to be briefer peas, so if you would like to place a few in your backyard, it is possible to purchase pea pods without needing to perform trellising. For indoor climbing, I enjoy them since they're refreshing, easy to develop, and flavor surprising once you flip them into pesto. Virtually any pea seed could be turned in to shoots, but so if you have any 'Sugar Snap' pea seed in your home, which will get the job done. I would avoid varieties created to be stable and tall, however, like 'Oregon Giant.'

- Sunflower: Though I have got a listing of sources at the close of the novel, I had intended to steer clear of mention of particular seed firms in the principal body of this book because I do not wish to appear biased. But here I will violate my rule since there isone company that offers exceptional sunflower seeds such as shoots, plus they are organic. Johnny's Selected Seeds, a firm from Maine that offers a pumpkin seed collection that is highly count - capable and very hearty. While I've tried other options, it has been disappointing, mainly if I have played about with growing out of sunflower seeds, which are usually intended for bird claws (I said gardening is an experience, right?). Stick with seeds intended for human consumption, also provide Johnny's an attempt.

- Popcorn: On a whim, we believed whether we could purchase organic popcorn in the co-op, sprout this, then plant it and then consume it shoots. As it happens, the solution is yes. Thus, you do not have to purchase "seed" from anywhere so long as you've got access to soda - corn kernels that are not processed, either coated in acrylic or salted at all. Popcorn is different from corn kernels since popcorn comes from particular strains of corn, which were cultivated with the intention. It means that you may have the ability to sprout corn and receive precisely the same effect. However, popcorn is much more reliable if you are attempting to develop shoots.

- Nasturtium: Among of the most common edible blossoms, nasturtiums make delicious shoots. As when placing in the backyard, nasturtiums could be somewhat slow to the fold. Consider soaking the seeds in warm water for one hour or more before dispersing them at the press.

Trays, Pots, and Other Containers

Much as with other kinds of microgreens, I tend to favor open-style seedling trays using nominal thickness and drainage slots at the base. The slots maintain the dirt from amassing an excessive amount of moisture, which may quickly cause mold within a shoots tray, despite adequate ventilation.

That is because the seeds have been sown so near each other, which with irrigation, root rot could develop into a problem within only twenty-five hours of planting. When selecting a pot or tray, maintain dirt use in mind. Due to these origins, the shoots do not require the sort of soil thickness you would notice with plant begins or indoor herb gardens. Conserve dirt by Selecting a bigger container, also make crop simpler with a pot or tray that is shallow instead of deeper. Though peas, sunflowers, and corn demand lots of distance in regards to root thickness, when implanted as shoots, even a challenging thing occurs: the origins start to curl into one another, developing a thick mat in the instance of pea shoots, also turning your plate to a good cube. I tend to utilize shallow trays only because of this, since weathered the dirt after the crop is readily achieved, such as throwing a tiny rug on the mulch pile. Bonus for homesteaders: cows adore the leftover stalks and seeds from holes. Therefore, you use minimum dirt, get maximum usage from the plate, and possibly even create your cows contented.

Prep perform

For passions, I discover a pure mulch combination will work nicely, so long as it is instead "fluffy" in a sense.

If all you've got is indoor potting soil, then lighten this up by incorporating vermiculite into the ground. The absolute most significant part of soil prep would be to bring some water into the mixture before planting, which helps to maintain moisture during the germination stage.

When mixing fertilizer and water, go to get a consistency that is just like a crumbly brownie combination --then get a few and squeeze. If a couple of drops of water come out, then that is perfect. When there's a continuous flow of water, then it means you have made the mix too moist, and you ought to add more dry mixture. It is not compulsory to premoisten the dirt in this manner, and I have put a lot of trays which did well without it; however, I have discovered it may accelerate germination time with a couple of days in case you use this technique. For seed preparation, there is a straightforward approach to accelerate the germination period: simply boil the seeds for approximately twenty-four hours before planting. Sometimes, particularly when the home feels over the colder side, that I yank them for a day or two more, so they start to sprout until I plant them. This can decrease germination up to a week in some instances.

However, be very careful about massaging during warm weather and for a lot longer than a lot of daylight hours because after they pass on the point where they are sprouting, they will begin to deteriorate and cannot be implanted. The worst aspect of needing to plant or placing it off for a long time would be the fact that rotting, moist shoots seeds give off a stench that can permeate the home. Seriously, it is among the worst stinks you could picture, such as fungus-crusted toe jam interior wet, filthy socks. Simply make it a point not to learn if I am characterizing that odor accurately.

Planting and Care First measures
Be sure that you begin with a fresh tray, grass, or alternative container, and include only a couple of inches of the soil mixture, ensuring to "up against it" if needed. Since the

mixture is moist, there is often a desire to push down the soil, but that produces a compaction problem that may turn your shoots into a hardened brick if it is placed under mild. Another factor when dispersing soil would be to have a little time to make a flat surface, particularly over the sides.

Regrettably, it's easy to Allow the dirt build up on both sides somewhat and return to some depression in the center; however, this accidental valley-like tray may lead to unevenness on your water supply, allowing a few seeds to sit down for a long time some dry outside. As soon as your soil mix is prepared, seed liberally. For shoots, which indicates you're going to be developing a seedbed in which the seeds seem too near together, but are not overlapping.

There is no need to poke holes in the dirt mixture and put seeds indoors, and they could sit together with the ground and develop perfectly well that manner. Bear in mind that every seed will develop a fire vertically; therefore, it is okay if they are all only a few fractions of an inch from one another, but you do not need them competing to get the specific same miniature stretch of dirt. Should you happen to sow them thicker and they are touching another in components, that is fine also, just understand that you may get less germination than ever anticipated.

The fantastic thing is these non-germinating seeds tend to find another chance after your first crop. Water quite lightly, then place a vacant black arrow on top of this micro arrow. This can help to keep the soil warm, also obstructing the light for a couple of days assists the seeds to become healthier generally.

You can glimpse indoors if you would like to observe the magical, but make sure you replace the cover when the seeds have not sprouted yet. As soon as they show any indication of expansion (approximately a few times), remove the water and cover every day. Put under lighting for eight hours daily. You're able to provide them a mix of natural light and sun if you are at a season or even a geographical area in which sunlight is sufficiently robust, but remember that the snaps will bend toward the light, therefore rotate the menu every day if needed. Otherwise, set the menu directly beneath your developing lights, approximately 6 inches in the tops of these plants.

Maintaining Growing

After they have established, shoots do not need much maintenance, and it can be a plus. But similar to microgreens, they profit considerably in the" floor watering" plan. Just fill out a kitchen sink, tub, another empty tray, together with approximately an inch of water, and also place the shoots into it for a couple of minutes. The plant will assume the water that it requires and moisturize the roots which way. This strategy is also helpful if shoots are appearing droopy and will need to replenish up.

In case you don't have a means to underside water, then water at the root level, or mist significantly rather than water. Shoots are just four season Plants (However, some period are far better than additional) if it is especially humid at home (summer in many instances) contemplate planting and replanting shoots just following the weather has cooled off. At Orientation River, we have attempted to develop shoots yearlong, and I have tried the same strategy in your home. However, there are unquestionably far better seasons than others concerningproductive growth.

Spring and autumn are perfect. With heat pads, winter brings slower expansion but plenty of shoots. Summertime, however, is barbarous for shoots in a home with central ac. If you don't adore playing with tweaking components continuously --warmth, more mowing, less mowing, underside watering, misting, much more airflow, more distinct positioning, etc.--I would suggest saving start growing for much more temperate seasons instead of summer.

Strategies for developing shoots

here are various additional tactics for maintaining your shoots track:

- keep watering and supplying light into the shoots menu following a very first crop. Many instances, a few seeds germinate afterward or are postponed since they are under new seeds. For pea shoots, particularly, you can have two to three additional harvests due to this. These following harvests will not be as plentiful as the very first ones, but they are enough to be well worth the attempt.
- In the event the atmosphere in your home appears mainly dry, mist the plants whenever they are in a young phase of expansion and then place a crystal clear tray at the top. These can be found at any garden shop, plus they help to allow in light but

- Lock moisture. I find those values in winter, mainly when the shoots are still merely from the germination point, but maybe not established sufficient yet. Alternately, it is also possible to use plastic wrap around, but just make individual the shoots are not increased enough to bump from the cap of the wrapping, which may slow down growth.

- Another fantastic tactic once the atmosphere is dry is to mist the plants more frequently throughout the day should they appear to be fighting. Be conscious that this technique can cause searing if the crops are near a natural light source, therefore increase the mild or reduce the crops by 6 inches and then mist greatly if that occurs.

Troubleshooting

Shoots Some typical issues and Possible solutions such as shoots:

No more Germination, even after a couple of Days
Shoots often germinate fast; therefore, this could be a significant matter. Above all, it is regarding the temperatures of the ground. Placing a cap within the tray will maintain the warmth and moisture indoors, but you want an excess boost, so look at placing the tray onto a heating mat that can be found at any garden shop. These rectangular mats increase the temperature slightly, just enough to allow the seeds to feel comfortable, but not sufficient to harm them to scorch your counter. It is possible to make it plugged into days if needed. When it's been a week, and you are not visiting germination,

assess the grade of your soil combination, and see whether it is overly tender -- compaction will frequently stop the seeds from launching.

Moldy Clumps within a Tray

Moldy clumps may be a consequence of improper airflow, overwatering, or even too much humidity. Whether there are untouched shoots from the menu, lift that segment (throw the moldy part) and move into another tray, allowing the soil to dry out a bit before you water. Wait a few days before picking to determine if mold grows with this section too;

In case it will discard and begin. In the event, the issue will be a lot of moisture from the beginning, which may occur during warm months, sow the seeds to dry dirt rather than pre-wetting the dirt mix, and also do a thorough watering before covering the groove during the germination procedure.

Cases of those Shoots Are Browning or Turning Dark

You've got them too near the light source, and that means you are cooking them at the tray. Move them away from your mild by another 6 inches, then clip off the hints mentioned above, and the rest will flourish.

Shoots Are Yellowing or Seeking Droopy Normally, and yellowing means overwatering, therefore allow your soil dry out a bit. By comparison, droopy fires are frequently brought on by under watering, or from a lot of humidity. If that's the circumstance, bottom water that the shoots in cold water and see whether they perk up after roughly ten to fifteen minutes.

Additionally, fix your buffs so that shoots are receiving some airflow to distribute stagnant, humid atmosphere and boost flow. Bear in mind that plants "breathe," and they want some warmth to maintain oxygen levels. If your attempts are not sufficient and the shoots continue being droopy, you might only need to harvest and consume --they will continue to be tasty and healthy, only a little less eloquent. Storage Factors Much like microgreens, shoots do most beautiful kept in glassand may last for weeks in the refrigerator in this manner. Pea shoots, even though fragile, are unusually long-lasting and maintain their crunch until the ending. Sunflower shoots are more stringent, and I have retained a few for three months in the refrigerator without

Any discernable shift in taste. Popcorn shoots, however, often last for some time and if retained for more, that strange aftertaste gets more powerful. So for all those, I might harvest and consume the identical moment.

Harvesting and Preservation

Getting Prepared to Choose for every Selection of shoots, There's a Perfect Time for the crop:

- Pea shoots these can develop long and seem unkind, and that I have a tendency to crop them if they are approximately 8 to 10 inches. If you'd like sweeter and much more uniform shoots, then harvest around 4 inches if they are just starting to unfurl their leaves. If you'd like a super-rich harvest, and also a pea-sweet flavor, then make them go till 12 inches. Longer than this, however, and they begin to get too heavy and long to get the tray, which means they begin flattening. Additionally, the taller they acquire, the further succulent the taste.

- Sunflower shoots these taste best once you buy them until the sunflowers create their first real leaves. In the shooting point, you will have two well crispy petals. If the first real leaves start tinkering, they develop involving those petals and possess a scratchy texture, which I do not like, although they're perfectly edible. Should you allow the shoots to opt for too long and the leaves begin coming up, then you are still able to delight in the shootsonly flavor and appear by plucking off the leaves that are true and shedding them. With regards to what to crop,

I clip all of the ways to the ground since the stalks are just as yummy as the leaves.

- Popcorn shoots. These are greatest at approximately 6 inches, and make sure you incorporate a number of those white-and-pink bottoms, in which the most extreme taste resides. When the shoots are becoming taller, they are fun to get from the windowsill only because they seem so lively, but the flavor grows increasingly more mountainous since they mature. At approximately ten inches, then the shoots have all of the taste and appeal of new lawn clippings.

Chapter 3
Herbs

Among the most gratifying jobs for almost any kitchen gardener is the herb kettle, brimming over with favorites such as sage or pops, or ripe using a medley of different mints. I have seen some Fantastic mixes collectively --such as making a "pasta sauce herb pot" with lavender, thyme, and basil-- because most herbs flourish from average harvest, they are ideal for a kitchen area because that you can just snip precisely what you will need for a specific dish. For my kitchen area, I love to place blossoms in separate baskets so I can isolate them from the event of pest problems or mold issues. However, I frequently produce mixes when giving herb baskets like gifts, and I love the scents that combine as a consequence of enabling them to appear collectively.

Generally, many blossoms have been well-geared toward indoor climbing, and many of those anglers I understand report their outside garden blossoms since the weather gets sharp so that they can expand the growing season inside. Many herbs, like rosemary, rosemary, thyme, and lavender, spread well if you choose a cutting out of a present indoor or outdoor plant and then prepare it for expansion indoors. If that is your plan, just cut on a 4-inch segment (measured from the tip of the stem/ foliage below the ground) and strip away about an inch or so of their reduced leaves. Set the stem to some potting mixture, like vermiculite, and maintain the mixture somewhat moist since the plant disappeared. These crops such as humidity, therefore, cover with transparent glass or plastic allowing light, however, trapping moisture but do not let them get too warm from sunlight. Additionally, eliminate their covers sometimes or set them onto a porch or "transitional" area to provide them some atmosphere. This technique works nicely for transplant bought at a greenhouse, which should be "hardened" to temperature variations.

In my experience, there are occasions when I simply cannot appear to grow particular herbaceous plants from seed (I am looking in the basil) and that I want the jumpstart a transplant could offer. As soon as I started my indoor climbing experiences, I depended on a transplant nearly entirely since I appreciated having the ability to bypass that first significant jump in germination. Nowadays, but I delight in the planting procedure, and tend to select herbs that flourish best in my kitchen. Therefore, for this particular section, we will have a better look at just how to select from seed to crop, and that means that you can find a sense of growing herbs entirely inside. Should you move the transplant or herb-cutting path, however, a lot of the data still applies, especially in regards to problems like soil temperatures and drainage.

Great Varieties for Indoor Growing

Though many herbs do attractively in an indoor expansion area, some forms can be unbelievably fickle if you are attempting to grow from seed. Here are some options, broken down by degree of difficulty:

Easy Like a Sunday Morning

- Peppermint and spearmint: Hearty and extensive, mint enjoys to invade the land of different crops, so as soon as you've obtained it, keep ahead of harvesting it. If You'd like a robust mint flavor without developing a Lot of it, then Elect for soda - mint, as It offers a more intense taste

- Lemongrass: You do not plant this one out of seed: simply purchase a stalk of lemongrass out of a grocery store or farmers' market, cut the shirt, and place the stem in a couple of inches of water. The stem will create roots by itself and heaps of fresh shoots, and you're able to harvest from them. *f* Exotic Steak: This number is known as more comfortable to develop than other types of hay. Also, it's as much taste.

- Additionally, it's quite significant and will last for weeks Requires Effort, but Ordinarily Doable

- Parsley: Normally rather simple to develop, but germination may be hit and miss. Typically, you are going to start to see expansion approximately two weeks following planting, and it tends to grow slower compared to other herbaceous plants generally.

- Oregano: The key using oregano is providing sufficient plant light daily; it might necessitate placing the marijuana beneath another bulb that is to get a couple of hours over the other blossoms. Typically, approximately eight hours of lighting is greatest *f* Thyme: This herb also needs more mild, so that I frequently place rosemary and thyme in precisely the same area or put them alongside each other at a window.

- Rosemary: I have discovered my indoor rosemary stems from slough off rosemary in my backyard, but additionally, it is somewhat simple to grow from seed. Look out for more overwatering, because rosemary will favor drier dirt, and Make Sure You choose a selection that works well with indoor climbing, such as 'Blue Spire

- Chervil: Quite uncommon, but very flavorful, chervil is linked to parsley and contains a subtle taste. The herb does nicely in low-light places, which makes it an incredible selection for kitchen corners and out-of-the-way stains, but remember it does not work nicely when temperatures start to grow beyond 70 degrees, so judge your home's temp before planting.

- Cilantro: Here is another one that develops remarkably well outdoors but demands a higher degree of maintenance inside. To start with, it does not transplant well. Therefore it has to be made from seeds or starter plants. Also, it takes lots of drainages and nonetheless needs more nourishment, which makes it hard to maintain the dirt nourished. It will do good after it is established, however until then, intend on providing the herb fertilizer biweekly, which is twice as far as the other herbaceous plants. Additionally, water only when the soil appears quite dry.

- Basil: It is so omnipresent in cooking, so you would think basil is a cinch to grow in your garden. However, no. Notoriously tough to grow indoors from seed, basil will function best as a plant begins out of a greenhouse. Additionally, these lush Italian Steak leaves might not be wide and reasonably as you possibly find in a backyard. Somewhat I lean toward types with smaller leaves such as 'Dark Opal' or even Thai basil.

- Sage: " It is not too tough to acquire sage began inside, but it is likely to pass with overwatering. There have been a lot of instances where I visit those thick leaves and believe the plant appears dry, and then I wind up killing it as it's already nicely ventilated. Additionally, many experts suggest waiting a very long time before picking while the plant becomes established--around a year sometimes. For me, the area in my kitchen growing region is too confined to nurse a plant, which takes weeks before I could use it, but I do like to get a little pot moving since the herb dries well after crop.

Soil Prep

Herbs are somewhat finicky when it comes to drainage. Many gardener intellectsare they "do not like wet feet," meaning that when their roots become too rancid, rust can result. Every plant kind covered in this publication (except nausea) depends upon appropriate drainage to a level, however for blossoms, it is particularly crucial since they are inclined to enjoy a humid environment, which makes them vulnerable to root rot. Merely utilizing a pot with holes at the bottom is not sufficient, and if you purchase a typical kind of marijuana using a dish that grabs water, then you are going to be in even more trouble. This frequently contributes to a plant sitting water, which is practically always a terrible position for your plant. There are lots of approaches that could be useful for raising drainage. Some anglers use a method made for developing cactus since these specialty combinations are intended to drain fast, but I discover that just blending sand and vermiculite (at the ratio of a one-to-four component) collectively tends to make a joyful mix.

In case you are transplanting from outdoors, do as far as possible to eliminate the current garden soil by lightly shaking or tapping on the roots. You will not have the ability to remove all the dirt, but if it is possible to get most of it, then you will significantly lower your exposure to backyard insects and diseases. Anything you use, a fantastic strategy to reduce compaction, is to nurture inside the pot each month approximately. You can simply Have a fork and lightly loosen the dirt inside the container, taking care to remain mainly on the periphery so that you don't harm the roots.

Trays, Pots, and Other Containers

At the risk of harping a lot on drainage, and I'm likely to highlight the value of drainage.I will also place it in italics in case it helps: drainage. Herbs simply don't succeed at all in almost any circumstance where they are sitting, therefore select a pot or container which enables ample flow. You can indeed try out growing cilantro on your midst school lunchbox or skillet in that repurposed table or another remarkable container appeals to you personally, but if you would like to maintain the herbs heading to get a significant long time, then drill several holes and perhaps even throw a few pebbles at the ground. Your herbaceous plants will probably thank you. Beyond this, any substance functions; however, I tend to shy away from terra cotta pots since they create the blossoms dry out quicker, which melts my estimation of how much watering they require. Due to limited space, I apologize toward smaller containers, but in case the herbs start to spread a lot over the borders, or I wish to invite them to get larger, I will repot into a bigger container.

Planting and Care First Measures

Having the container and dirt blend prepared, and provide the mix a few glasses of water so that it's slightly moist. This helps your seeds from changing when you water them. Sow the seeds about a few times more durable than the magnitude of this seed. That is a rule of thumb, and that which is generally meant for me is that if it is a teensy little seed, then I will barely push it in the ground, then I'll cover it with only a bit of vermiculite. When the seeds are more prominent, I would press half an inch and cover it. Water gently, then cover the container or pot with plastic kitchen

Wrapping. This is going to keep the soil seed and mix hot, to promote germination. Set the container or pot in a bright place or below a mild, and once the seedlings emerge, then remove the plastic wrap.

Maintaining Growing

Some herbs need specialized attention, but Generally Speaking, most may benefit from these suggestions for maintaining erections going strong:

- Fertilize every ten days or so with diluted fish mulch,

located in any garden shop. At a pinch, I have also soaked rosemary in warm water for a couple of hours, allow it to cool, then sprayed that onto the crops. However, for this to be more "at a pinch" strategy, you would need to be among those Men and Women who appear to possess dried seaweed from the cabinet.

- Herbs such as humidity, but it is not always simple to tweak this illness, particularly in the summer months. One good strategy is to produce a tray of little stones or pebbles and then fill the tray with water, leaving approximately 1/4 inch of the best dry. Set the pots in addition to the trays making sure they do not touch the water, and the evaporation procedure will help to maintain the atmosphere at a beautiful humidity level.

- Give blossoms a routine "tub" by misting every couple of days. Does this help keep your hydrated, but also, it cuts down to pest issues because diminished plants are more susceptible to insects such as aphids and spider mites?

- Water at the bottom of this herb, not just leaves. This will enable the plant to become hydrated, without having it too "flattening out" from an excessive amount of water hitting on the leaves.

Troubleshooting

Herbaceous One of the common issues and Possible solutions for herbaceous plants:

Slow Growth or Limited Germination

Potentially, this might be a mild matter. Herbs need five or more hours of light each day to remain healthy, and full-size sunshine (given that the place is not overly hot) is best. However, in winter, even just a south-facing window may be inadequate. If you see slow growth, consider expanding the time in which the herbs are below mild up to two hours if needed.

Brown Patches or even Withered-Looking Candles When your herbs are beneath a light source, they could be too near the bulb. Mostly, you're burning.Herbs

Ought to be 6 to 8 inches from the light source, which space will be measured from the bulb into the peak of the plant.

Whitish Fuzz on Soil

This may be organic seed germination, but it might also be mold. Confirm that you are not overwatering--should you place your finger to the soil mixture and sense moisture instantly, then that may be the situation. Allow the plant "dry " and isolate it in the other crops in the meantime. Eliminate the moldy places, but bear in mind you might want to begin with this one.

Stems Seem Soft or Mushy

This could be an additional prevalence of overwatering. Stems often feel soft when root corrosion is happening. Another significant sign of issues is that a filthy odor mixed with all the beautiful herb aromas.

Bug Infestation at Progress

It is so disheartening to lean over a kettle of herbs, prepared to snip off a couple of choices for supper, and see something else is before you at the buffet.If it comes to pass, isolate the plant and then attempt a soap spray. This is a mixture of gentle liquid soap (such as Dr. Bronner's) along with also water. Spray in the day since the program once the plant remains in sunlight may cause bleeding.

Harvesting and Preservation

Getting prepared to decide on Each herb is chosen in its way, but generally speaking, go to the "old" leaves, which are complete. Start looking for new development, typically close to the middle of this plant, also prevent clipping near that region as you don't wish to shorten the life span of this herb. When your plant begins to blossom, snap the flowering area Once Possible to lengthen the plant's interval --such as many crops, herbs start flowering for a sign they're done growing (it is a procedure referred to as "bolting"). By taking away the flowers, you're able to fool the plant to sticking around for more essentially. When picking, remember that stalks often possess abundant flavor too. For example, cilantro stalks are equally as intensely flavored because of the leaves.

Storage Concerns

Because of a current homesteading kick, I have been experimenting with several strategies to conserve virtually everything, from roasted cabbage into dried celery.

In comparison to trying to conserve artichokes, blossoms are a breeze. There are many strategies to be confidentyour herbs may last for weeks. The fastest method is via drying-- easily create a package, strip about an inch of leaves to expose just stalks, tie with twine or even a rubber ring, and hang in a cool, moist location. There is a part of my cellar which smells quite remarkable at this time, as a result of numerous capsule packages. The Benefit of drying will be that you can depart the packages hanging for very some time, or only crumble them whenever they are dehydrated and set them into jars. Another storage option would be preservation in olive oil. Be sure the glass jar is extremely dry, then fill it with herbs such as peppermint, thyme, and peppermint, in addition to some other ingredients such as garlic. Fill the jar with olive oil, making sure the oil fully covers the blossoms, also in approximately fourteen days, the petroleum is going to be infused with taste.

Following that, it is possible to strain the herbs and then drizzle the brand new generation over anything you enjoy. In the same way, you can finely chop herbs, set them in a glass jar, and cover entirely with honey. In fourteen days, the taste will infuse the honey, and in this scenario, I do not attempt to strain the herbs out. This mixture may be utilized instead of jam on toast, or even a few folks only eat a spoonful whenever they are feeling energy drained, mainly if more herbal herbs are traditionally utilized. In general, herbaceous plants are a leading addition to any kitchen garden, also integrating just a couple of favorites might help enhance the tastes of your meals. Now, I am irritatingly snobby in regards to "new" herbs whom I see in the supermarket because they seem so exhausted and exhausted. Knowing my herbs are chosen just about ten minutes until I love these makes me feel nostalgic, particularly in the winter, after this amount of freshness could be quite so tough to reach otherwise.

Chapter 4
Sprouts

When you are short on resources and space, sprouts create a simple indoor climbing endeavor. Essentially, you simply need seeds, a glass jar (more on this shortly), a few cheesecloths, or a thin dishtowel and sew! You are on your way into getting a sprout specialist. Nutritionally, sprouts can also be packed with fiber, enzymes, amino acids, vitamins, antioxidants, and other snacks, which help enhance your immune system and maintain your wellbeing on track. Additionally, they are delicious and rather straightforward to develop consistently. I tend to undertake a more rapid growing session at the depths of the winter, when other crops may be slowing within their progress. At a Minnesota February, even microgreens will take more time to turn out of seed to lush green carpeting. Therefore sprouts assist me in receiving a nutritional supplement while I am waiting.

Not all Sprouts allure to me personally in terms of flavor, however, and it is very likely you'll make the same discovery I enjoy sprouts using a kick like a peppermint or mustard, but people with a more earthy flavor (such as alfalfa) aren't my groove. And that is okay since there are loads of options when it comes to selecting which kind of sprouts to increase, and discover everything you enjoy is a portion of this sprouting adventure.

Great Varieties for Indoor Growing

There are lots of options in regards to sprouting, and similar to microgreens, they encircle a substantial chunk of the vegetable kingdom. It's possible to sprout dill seeds, fenugreek, chives, legumes, wheat germ, and a lot of other people. Since you get more confident in your sprout installation, you can play with various options, and however, in terms of getting started, these are a few popular options:

- Alfalfa: This is the timeless sprout, using light and nutty flavor. Also, it creates a pleasant starting point for sprouting.

- Broccoli: Research at Johns Hopkins University reported that broccoli sprouts also pose an "exceptionally abundant supply of inducers of enzymes that protect against chemical compounds." Plus: yummy.

- Mung bean: lots of kinds of beans can be sprouted, and that is among the very jazzy. I am not fond of the flavor, but I have talked to folks who eat them daily and locate them creamy and yummy.

- Blends: If you shop on the internet for sprouts in places like Sprout- people.com, then you will come across quite a few combinations with some kinds of seeds, and it is almost always an excellent option. For example, an "Italian Combination" will couple clover, garlic, and cress, or even a grain mixture might consist of wheat, rye, oats, Kamut, and quinoa. These are typically an extremely cost-effective approach to buy multiple kinds of seeds without purchasing them separately.

- Others: In principle, you can sprout any seed that you desire. In practice, some only taste better compared to many others. Besides another sprout with this particular page, seed catalogs and merchants promote a number of these following: fenugreek, daikon radish, edamame legumes, spinach, sunflower, buckwheat, and onions.

Trays, Pots, and Other Containers

There are lots of options in regards to abundant sprout development, and take a look at the Resources page at the rear of the book for several excellent websites to search for supplies. If you anticipate developing sprouts frequently, look at obtaining a sprouter. These devices vary from a tiny, cup-like container that is generally around $10 into some multitray sprouted, which allows you to develop multiple kinds of sprouts concurrently. This bigger sprouter may be enjoyable, making little sprout skyscrapers on your kitchen, but remember you'll want to keep together with this procedure in case you've got multiple sprout kinds growing on various timeframes.

Sprouts are not hard to develop. However, they do need particular care completed at fixed intervals, and therefore unlike shoots or perhaps microgreens, you cannot begin them and go off for a couple of days. But if you are turning right into a sprout enthusiast along with your counter is consumed with too many containers and jars, a multitray sprouter might be precisely what you want. But if you are only getting started and you also wish to experiment using only one sprout variety at one moment, then reevaluate your installation by using just a glass jar (I use a quart-sized Mason or even Ball jar) plus a few cheesecloths or a thin dishtowel for putting over the surface. The sprouting seeds will probably require some airflow but will probably be allergic to dust, therefore refrain from having a milder lid because it can trap moisture.

Prep Work

First, ensure your jar or sprouter remains clean. And I am clean. Sprouts are already vulnerable to mold difficulties, and thus don't have an opportunity by believing a few dried flecks of meals or any dust will not be a significant thing. You do not have to bleach out the container but require a few minutes to test it thoroughly after washing and be sure it's prepared. When searching containers for sprouting, I favor hand-washing them to utilizing my dishwasher since I believe they make a much better scrub like that.

Planting and Care First Steps

Place about a tablespoon of seeds on your jar or container and cover them with

A couple of inches of hot water. I tend to work with filtered water because I find that I get much better results this way, but occasionally use tap water when I am in a hurry. Listed below are steps out of there:

- Permit the seeds to soak overnight, up to twenty-five hours if you are sprouting bigger seeds such as beans.
- In the morning, or after the boil, drain All the water, instead, although the cheesecloth, therefore, it acts as a

filter.

- Fill the jar with a few more inches of clean water, and then drain through the filter.
- Put in place with indirect lighting.
- Place in water, and now set the jar back in your counter.
- Duplicate this procedure --drain, simmer to wash, drain, fill with water every morning and day (every twelve months, approximately) for the subsequent four to six weeks, before the sprouts have become a point where you are all set to crop them.
- Before ingestion, provide the sprouts last beverage, and get up to from these as possible. Then you can just set the jar in the fridge.

Troubleshooting

Some typical issues and potential remedies for nausea:

Flu Types from the Jar

Of all of the issues with sprouts, here can be the biggest. You truly have to remain on top of this rinsing program, since otherwise, you are going to get a mushy, moldy mess and might need to begin. If this comes to pass, throw the carrots out (even when they have got a tiny mold patch) and begin again, make sure you sterilize the jar until you do. If the issue keeps occurring, look at employing a separate container to the sprouting, like a sprouter or even a tray.

Sprouts Seem to Be Taking over Six Days

In case you are living in a chilly climate, then sprouts may take somewhat longer to reach adulthood. It's possible to accelerate the procedure by soaking the seeds overnight before putting them at a sprouter or jar. This will aid the seeds to germinate quicker. Additionally, you can decide on a sprouting type, which is going to be on a quicker schedule, such as beans. This class contains kidney beans, adzuki beans, cowpeas, garbanzos, and legumes. Beans frequently take just approximately two to four times from multiplying to adulthood.

Sprouts Are Increasing, but Do Not appear to Make "Greening Up."

Even though sprouts are useful within a place with indirect lighting, occasionally, they require an increase of photosynthesis. If your sprouts aren't getting green, then move the container into a place with more magnificent lighting, or near a window. Just be sure it is not in direct sun, because that may dry the carrots out. Additionally, remember that not all sprouts will be more green. For example, mung beans are a fairly, translucent white when fully sprouted, using a yellowed hint that results in the seed husk.

Harvesting and Preservation Getting prepared to Pick

If you "crop" sprouts, then it merely means that you pull them from their glass container and then consume them. What can be simpler? Just ensure they pass the smell test-- also when I have eaten out of a jar of sprouts, I will smell them before placing them in my salad. That is, as there are frequent warnings regarding sprouts being correlated with outbreaks of Salmonella and E. coli, that may take place if the sprouts have been permitted to sit for a long time. When that happens, bacteria may form, and also the tender sprouts are more vulnerable.   I have discovered that smelling the carrots before eating averts problems. If they're off whatsoever, the odor is detectable, in my own experience. When in doubt, always throw it away.

Storage Concerns

Sprouts do not keep well, and also, if you place the jar from the fridge, the maximum shelf life you are likely to have would be about weekly. Then, that may be pushing it. The sprouts will start to demonstrate corrosion by getting somewhat mushy, and until long mold will shape. The best strategy with sprouts would be to eat them within a couple of days once they are fully grown.

Chapter 5
Mushrooms

Just a little Forest Right in Your Countertop

For me, mushrooms have just a small bit of puzzle. Perhaps it's because I grew up eating just the salty, salty mushrooms which came sliced, thrown into a pumpkin. The only new mushroom experiences I had as a child would be the occasional fleck at a can of cream of mushroom soup--and believe me, and if you reside in the Midwest, you are very likely to eat the fat in cream of mushroom soup, because it creates the base of roughly 75% of potluck dishes (the remainder is Jell-O). Thus, when I eventually ate "actual" mushrooms as an adult, this is a sin. Nowadays, I search out exotic mushrooms and Conquer men and women who forage to them. Additionally, once you're standing in the co-op and taking a look at the astronomical cost of morels, you most likely say, "Who'd pay that much for mushrooms" The solution is. It appears plausible that I would be eager to grow indoors, and I have made many efforts to maintain a vast selection of mushrooms, but tell the truth, there are just a few forms that do the job nicely (see the types section for more information) within my own space.

I have attempted to maintain logs grapple with shiitake spawn in my cellar, but it can be quite tricky to maintain humidity and humidity amounts ideal if you are attempting to grow out of logs inside. Let us have a few simpler avenues instead.

Get Prepared

Great Media for Indoor Growing When choosing which kind of mushroom that you would like to increase, it is crucial to choose spawn (that is what mushroom "newcomer" is known as) that functions nicely with whatever medium you have selected. For example, oyster mushrooms grow best in capsules, while wine caps succeed in sawdust. When making a decision, select your moderate first, then find out precisely what mushrooms grow nicely inside. Here's a quick cheat sheet:

Sawdust: The advantage of utilizing sawdust is it's cheap, and you will generally purchase tiny bags of it in a garden shop. Make sure you acquire the fine-grained sawdust instead of the substance that is nearer to woodchips. The mushrooms that perform well in this medium are all shiitake and wine limit.

Straw: Since it retains moisture but also allows for a beautiful quantity of warmth, straw is a beautiful medium for mushrooms, broccoli, and oyster mushrooms to develop exceptionally well in capsules. There are lots of sorts of straw. However, wheat germ will be very best for growing.

Hardwood block: A good option for first-time thieves is that a "table upper farm," that functions as a part of an abysmal log, or comprised within a wooden sawdust block. You merely should water, fix humidity levels as educated, and appreciate. These cubes have restricted fruiting occasions, unlike the number of that spawn increased in straw or sawdust, but they also generally have more exceptional success prices. You buy pre-inoculated logs for about $30-$40: those can yield a dozen approximately shiitakes everythree weeks when the fruiting starts. Or you can inoculate your log or logs using shiitake spawn.

One factor to remember when ordering is That Lots of mushroom spawn providers will only ship through specific days of the year. For example, leading provider Field & Forest may send mushroom kits just from November till May, though it does send certain kinds of spawn year-round. Moreover, make sure to buy spawn rather than spores. It is possible to utilize dyes (which are like seeds) for indoor climbing, instead of spawn, which will be similar to purchasing transplants with origins formed, but it requires quite a little expertise, patience, time to develop out of spores.

Prep Work

When you are using a straw for a mushroom moderate, here is where it is going to find a bit bizarre. Decrease the odds of disease difficulties, it is ideal for pasteurizing the straw, and therefore, you have to nourish it. I am not kidding. Set a large pot of water in the stove, allow it to boil for about twenty minutes as you're chopping down the straw to a manageable dimension, typically approximately 1 to 3 inches. I usually just grab a few straws, take it over a bowl and then cut it with scissors I purchase 2-inch strands. Many folks use a blender or food processor; however, I have discovered the cleanup with that process to be overly time-consuming.

Once the water has been boiling for some time, reduce the

temperature to just beneath a boil, then also use a meat thermometer to check the water, which ought to be between 160 and 170 degrees Fahrenheit. After that, insert the straw into the water, and then induce any drifting straw (there'll be a lot) below the water using a skillet. Ideally, all of the straw should stay beneath the water, so if you can, burden the straw, which has a little grate, Pyrex dish, or even alternative heat-resistant product. Continue checking the warmth of this water to be sure it remains within reach and "cook" the straw for approximately 45 minutes. After that, switch off the cooker, allow the sew fresh for approximately ten minutes, then drain the water out of the kettle. Do not throw the water away. You can utilize it "straw juice" to your mushrooms after, providing them a nutrient kick.

Eliminate the straw out of the bud, allow it to come to room temperature before spawning. It will Start to dry; however, it is useful to possess the straw to be moist after presenting the spawn. You might even get a pasteurized straw, but where is the fun in that? In this manner, your kitchen may odor "army" to get no less than a day or two.

Planting and Care First Measures
Wash your hands along with the prep area thoroughly. Mushroom spawn is vulnerable to illness, and using a sterile environment is especially important. Shred your straw or evenly disperse your sawdust on your container, then mix in a few used coffee grounds. If you are a tea drinker, then it is worthwhile to pop up right into a nearby coffee shop and Request a small bucket of reasons --they generally throw them

off anyway, and many stores close to urban gardening attempts are utilized to all those kind of orders.

The coffee grounds are packed with enzymes that supply a significant boost to a mushroom spawn, and besides, they help reduce the number of germs that may compete with your spawn. Your spawn will generally seem like a block of quite old cheese. Break this up in very tiny crumbles and incorporate it with all the straw or sawdust. Sometimes, the spawn will probably be from sawdust, and that means you merely need to add it into another, thicker coating of the substance. Concerning a container, then you may use many different containers, but among the most well-known approaches is to package a plastic bag using the moderate and spawn, then poke holes in it every 3 inches or so. This will permit airflow while keeping the entire package rancid and warm. Alternately, you can use a plate or baking pan and then spread the mix evenly, which Provides the mushrooms more space to grow. Distribute some potting soil on the surface, then mist completely. Set the pan or bag in a cool, dark place, including a cellar. You might even utilize a garage provided that the temperature is about 50 degrees Fahrenheit. Mist the mix periodically if it appears like it is beginning to become dry. You may start to observe a whitish fuzz grow --do not worry, it is not molded. For mushrooms, mold is probably to be black, yellow, pink, or bluish-green.

Troubleshooting

Some typical issues and potential remedies for mushrooms:

No First Growth Occurring

This could occur once an area is too trendy, or you do not have sufficient moisture. If you have been misting the mushrooms regularly, consider placing a germination mat below your container. In the event the challenge is moisture, then consider setting a moist towel above the container for a couple of days so that moisture could be included better. Do not leave it for a long time, however, because the mushrooms require a little fresh air to reduce carbon dioxide buildup.

Multiple Mushroom Growing Efforts:with no Results

Perhaps you have tried both straw and sawdust, you have altered your containers, attempted different rooms at home and corners of the cellar, possibly even sung into the spawn. And you're getting nothing. Sadly, this sometimes happens even with temperatures and moisture control. In cases like this, you might choose to put money into indoor gardener apparel. I guarantee this is not cheating. These kits are extremely well created for climbing and frequently assemble with mycologists (mushroom specialists) that are super informed about making options for indoor surroundings. Opt for a kit that is either one of those "tabletop plantation" types, or

Only an easy tote full of spawn and sawdust (occasionally with java thrown) that just has to be watered at regular intervals.

Harvesting and Preservation

Getting Ready to Harvest

Based on the number, mushrooms must be all set for a while

at around three weeks. Typically, the best indication of adulthood is the caps will probably separate from the stalks. At that point, just select them.

Storage Concerns

Do not wash the mushrooms until you are prepared to prepare them for a meal; this can let them survive longer. Place them in a brown paper bag (not in plastic), and Shop in the refrigeratetor. A plastic container can trap moisture, whereas the newspaper bag absorbs any extra moisture coming from the mushrooms. Should you have to shop eggs for more, look at dehydrating them cook them, and freeze them.

Chapter 6
Lettuce

Radishes, Carrots, Tomatoes, and Other Compounds Many plants using a shallow root system may grow well inside, like beets, radishes, a few forms of carrots, lettuces, also with the ideal requirements, even hot tomatoes and peppers. With these kinds of plants, it is more important to set up proper growing methods as outlined in Part One of the book--appropriate airflow, a solid indoor dirt mix, artificial light, insect prevention, and proper containers. Having a designated growing place setup correctly, the fun could start. Although growing mini-crops such as pea shoots is a jaunty project, I find a deep pride in cultivating indoor vegetables, which take the time to create, rewarding me with a plate full of lush salad greens, sweet carrots, peppery radishes, and another bounty in my kitchen garden. Particularly in the spring, even when I am craving new greens, however, just locate West Coast (or globally sent) options in my supermarket, I feel motivated to select a planting frenzy, filling every available area with shelves, lighting, along with just-seeded pots. Perhaps not every vegetable is ideal for my kitchen countertops, however. I have tried many types which may start alright but lack the dirt thickness necessary, or that prosper better outside within the specialty.

Here, we will cover different types of plants which produce the best sense for indoor climbing, and have a peek at specific factors concerning soil, pest avoidance, containers, along with the light. Much like the groundwork for faster-growing plants such as microgreens and pea shoots, effectively developing and harvesting of indoor plants is about the excellent upfront job, paying attention, and preserving that all-important awareness of experience.   Lettuces Before I started farming, then " I had been a salad type of woman. That tag evolved over the years, however: rising, "salad" has been a wedge of iceberg lettuce with ranch dressing and another person (we will sidestep the reality that at Minnesota, "salad" is also Jell-O and Cool Whip), but finally I made my way to a Massive variety of greens,

Such as red oak leaf, butterhead, Bibb, and romaine. I like the mix of textures and colours it's possible to place together with salad combinations, particularly with options such as the 'Freckles' collection that develops with profound splashes of red or 'hazes," which creates tight minds of reddish leaves that conceal a good lime green Centre.

There are many options when it has to do with lettuce variety it just sounds right to kick the plants chapter with this flexible and much- adored vegetable.

Get Prepared Fantastic Varieties for Indoor Growing

At the risk of oversimplifying the array of lettuce options, I will make a general promise: lettuce will come in among two variations --you have head lettuce that is accurate to this definition, or you've got salad combinations that combine lots of varieties and develop in a cluster as opposed to a tightly contained mind. That does not indicate they're two different types--mind lettuces could be contained in a mixture, you merely harvest them if they are still little greens. The gap comes through the seeding process since you space them to adapt for head lettuce expansion in these kinds, or you also seed liberally (although not as significantly as

Microgreens) so which you may harvest several types concurrently. If it comes to indoor climbing, I almost always gravitate into the mixtures because they grow fast, I will seed them based on color dimensions, and they feature a selection of tastes out of mustard greens along with peppery arugula to moderately 'Rouge d'Hiver' and frilly'Lollo Rosso.' Many seed Businesses market their combinations. However, you can also create your own out of contenders like those:

- Arugula: Also called the rocket, this is a reliable alternative for including a peppery taste to sandwiches. The spiky, dark green leaves blend well in a salad but,besides, may be substituted for salmon in individual dishes.

- Green Oakleaf' and 'Red Oakleaf': Maybe Not surprisingly, all these lettuces receive their title for having leaves, which are much like those of pine trees. In cases like this, oak leaf is an umbrella word with various types in that household, for example, as 'Tango," 'Bolsachica,' "Panisse,' and my favorite, 'Sulu' (that I adore because I am a sci-fi nerd). Oakleaf varieties are straightforward to develop and have a tendency to get a mild taste and crunch.

- Baby foliage: Similar to oak leaf, "baby foliage" is a general expression as opposed to a number inside itself. Made to be chosen from a young period of expansion, a few excellent selections for baby leaf lettuce "Red Sails,' "Refugio,' "Parris Island," and 'Defender.' Following is a head's up for seed trimming: a few infant foliage options will also be oak leaf types, but not all of oak leaf options are designated as infant foliage and confused yet? Do not worry--that the designation does not matter for developing, it is only a means to suggest which lettuces are greatest if harvested in a tiny stage.

- Lollo Rosso': Incredibly frilly and somewhat sour, this lettuce comes with an intense flavor that gets stronger as it becomes more prominent. The reddish leaves have a glowing green splash close to the floor, and it is inclined to be highest when blended with milder lettuces instead of served.

There are numerous types of lettuce, which is an issue of visual and taste preference concerning what you select. I tend to enjoy a little bit of peppery taste, a hint of bitterness, along with a range of greens and reds. If you prefer just mild greens, then elect for one variety that guarantees that color and flavor.

Should you cannot decide and just need several seed types mixed, then select one of those carrot mixes offered from the seed companies which specialize in people. Regardless of what you decide, I would suggest jotting down notes that are growing in a diary. When developing many types of lettuce, then I occasionally forget that which works well and what does not or that which tasted too sour or too dull. A fast perusal of the gardening diary before ordering regularly helps to differentiate the bountiful in the blah.

Trays, Pots, and Additional containers

Because lettuce has a shallow root system, so it also functions nicely within a medium-sized container. I tend to work with hanging baskets since I will move them more efficiently, and since they look beautiful as a focus inside the kitchen, particularly if I am climbing lettuces with loads of crimson leaves. As with other crops, lettuce will perform better in vinyl compared to at terra cotta pots, since the clay will dry out the ground blend quicker compared to plastic. If you enjoy the look of terra cotta, simply pop up a plastic insert into bud. Just be sure that there are holes at the bottom for proper drainage.

Soil Mix

As long as you are not using dirt from the backyard, lettuces can flourish in many different land types. You do not need to play about with drainage options by adding stones or mixing sand into a mulch mix --simply grab a purse of all-purpose potting mixture, and you are all set. The combination ought to be designated and organic for vegetable growth.

Planting and Care First Steps

Fill the pot with dirt, with approximately an inch of distance between the top of the container along with the ground. Sprinkle the carrot seeds in addition to the ground, taking care to divide any which are close to one another. To get a medium-sized bud, you're likely going to use about twenty-five seeds. However, it is not vital to become picky about it and then rely on them out. You do not have to find worried about feeling, possibly, provided that they are not clumped together.

Maintaining Growing

When the lettuces Start to launch, There Are Numerous methods for fostering expansion:

- Water every day to keep the ground moist but not soaked. The Best Way to tell if it needs water is to put your finger around half of an inch into the ground and if it feels dry, water.

- Since lettuces get more prominent, it is generally far better to base water. This usually means filling a bin or sink with a couple of inches of water and then putting the carrot bud into it for approximately ten minutes. Do not Allow the lettuce sit for Quite a While, or accumulate water at a plate below the kettle; this may cause root rot.

- You will observe that many lettuces are sprouting from precisely the same location. Weed from the more reduced energies so the more powerful ones could have more space to expand. When the weeded-out seedlings Appear workable in Any Way, simply transfer them into another pot or consume them because of microgreens.

- Fertilize if expansion looks slow. I do not usually utilize fertilizer to get lettuces because they do not often need the increase, but in case your lettuces are trying to find they might use some Excess nourishment, use a compost once per week for three weeks and see whether this makes a huge difference. Do not use over that, however, or you can "burn" the plant via over-fertilization.

Troubleshooting

It's Been a Week, and There Is No Germination

In case you have been watering gently and providing the lettuces sunlight, then be patient and wait for a second week; occasionally, in certain circumstances, they are sometimes sluggish concerning germination but can prove fine as soon as they begin growing. When it's been a couple of weeks, and there is no germination, then you could be overwatering or placing the bud in a place that is too dim.

The Lettuces Seem Droopy

One of the pleasant things about living in the Midwest is that lettuces do well inside because a lot of this year is trendy (perhaps a bit too much of this year for some people). Lettuce enjoys cooler temperatures and also will flourish most at approximately 60 to 70 degrees Fahrenheit. If you are experiencing higher temperatures or humidity inside your property, consider transferring the lettuce into a more relaxed place.

Harvesting and Preservation Getting prepared to Pick

Harvesting lettuces is a cinch --simply snip them at any given stage of expansion appeals to you. Typically, I favor smaller lettuce greens instead of bigger leaves, so that I cut them if they are just about 6 inches. Regardless of what size you pick, just make sure to prevent the internal leaves of each cluster, because it includes the immature expansion that will cause your next salad.

Storage Factors

Like microgreens, lettuce will maintain the best in containers. Also, they do good in plastic bags put in the crisper drawer of the fridge. Generally, however, it is far better to harvest just what you will need for a specific meal and allow the plant to retain producing lettuce leaves.

TIPS AND TRICKS FOR MICROGEREENS CULTIVATION

Sprouting on a counter, microgreens are an indication of life when you are desperate for a few green. Elegant because garnishes, filled with flavors and zesty notes, also a windowsill harvest of microgreens tastes of spring. And also for the gardener who likes to cook? Mini sprouts move from seed to salad in under 14 days.

1. Locate a bright windowsill.

A southern environment, in which light pops, "provides you stronger crops, with greater taste, color, and longer shelf life" Should you reside in Southern California, as Fitzpatrick does, then expand them outside.

2. Do not overlook drainage.

Pick a menu at least 1.5 inches deep, with empty holes.

3. Utilize a seed starting mixture.

A fluffy, lightweight dirt, such as EB Stone's Seed Starter Mix, can help tiny sprouts develop. Fill out a plate with 1 inch of seed starting mixture and completely wet the dirt so it is moist (not dripping) in the outside to the ground.

4. Think past lettuce.

"I love sunflower microgreens, however there is plenty of interesting things on the market, such as radish, dull bok, bok choi, red amaranth, arugula, lettuce, and mustard greens," says Fitzpatrick.

5. Scatter seeds around one-eighth into a quarter inch apart.

"It is not a specific science, and therefore don't be worried if you end up over-seeding. I discover more is far better than," says Fitzpatrick. Cover the seeds evenly using a different half-inch coating of seedling mixture and moist down that too.

6. Jump fertilizer.

Microgreens are in reality cotyledon leaves, meaning they are the first ones to moan following germination. They want only water and sun to develop. Based upon the seeds, then you may notice sprouting shoots at three to five times.

7. Mist, and do not overwater.

Heavy watering can crush seedlings or lead to mould to grow in the dirt.

8. Harvest.

Many microgreens will be prepared for harvest in 10 to 14 days. Cut them in clusters only above the soil line. Drink cold water and consume.

9. Repeat.

Once you crop, microgreens don't grow back again. For a constant supply, it is possible to reuse the soil by turning it on. Sprinkle seeds, and then cover with another layer of dirt. The origins in the former crop will have produced a mat which will gradually mulch itself," says Fitzpatrick, "therefore it is all very self-sustaining."

Conclusion

Inside this publication, I have covered several options that have been effective for me with gardening, but finally, it is going to be your responsibility to play with your mixture of raw projects. Perhaps you'll develop carrot microgreens rather than carrots, or you will focus just on lettuces since you and your pet bunny both love a just-harvested plate of greens. Watch every achievement as a chance to start the door only a bit longer, and understand that the ability of reverses. Occasionally --more frequently than I would enjoy, surely --I will embark on a strategy that does not get the job done, and I am back to feeling boggling. However, I simply write down the results of my experiments and continue to alternative options. Can the 'White Beauty' radish differ? Can I pull a watermelon radish, although it's much bigger than what I have implanted previously? These are the sorts of questions that render me looking bright and diverted when I am standing in line in the greenhouse, purchasing greater coconut coir or fish compost option. I have come to love these daydream minutes since it implies that I am still interested and open to the advertisement venture.

In gardening, and particularly in indoor gardening using its catchy nuances, it can be simple to feel defeated occasionally. Despite all of my cheerleading throughout this publication, I have experienced lots of frustration once I see mold, aphids, or even crumpled leaves. The toughest moments are the ones when I glance at a pot of dirt mix and understand that there is supposed to be quite a small sweet sprout poking through vermiculite, and I have nothing. However, I comfort myself with the recognition that this is a work-in-progress, which adaptability and versatility are characteristics to notify not just my gardening, but also my perspective on virtually everything. While I believe that way,I visit my small indoor garden for a sign of everything I would like to nurture in my entire life: nutrition, attention, awareness, and happiness. Revel in that burst of gratification that accompanies watching a plant start to sprout from the ground, and love that sense as it conveys all of the ways into the minute that you serve it within a meal. In lots of ways, us, it not only produces a link between our meals but also on our communities and our world.

www.ingramcontent.com/pod-product-compliance
Lightning Source LLC
Chambersburg PA
CBHW070552160726
48003CB00005B/2020